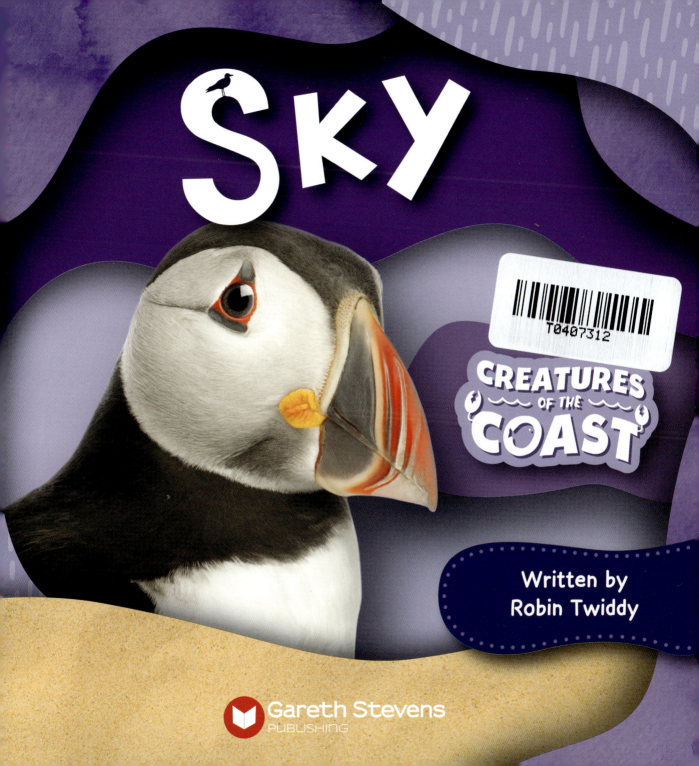

SKY

CREATURES OF THE COAST

Written by
Robin Twiddy

Gareth Stevens
PUBLISHING

Please visit our website, www.garethstevens.com. For a free color catalog of all our high-quality books, call toll free 1-800-542-2595 or fax 1-877-542-2596.

Published in 2025 by
Gareth Stevens Publishing
2544 Clinton St.
Buffalo, NY 14224

Written by:
Robin Twiddy

Edited by:
Rebecca Phillips-Bartlett

Designed by:
Amy Li

Cataloging-in-Publication Data

Names: Twiddy, Robin.
Title: Sky / Robin Twiddy.
Description: New York : Gareth Stevens Publishing, 2025. | Series: Creatures of the coast | Includes glossary and index.
Identifiers: ISBN 9781538294741 (pbk.) | ISBN 9781538294758 (library bound) | ISBN 9781538294765 (ebook)
Subjects: LCSH: Sea birds--Juvenile literature.
Classification: LCC QL678.52 T837 2025 | DDC 598.177--dc23

© 2023 Booklife Publishing

This edition is published by arrangement with Booklife Publishing

All rights reserved. No part of this book may be reproduced in any form without permission in writing from the publisher, except by a reviewer.

Printed in the United States of America

CPSIA compliance information: Batch #CSGS25: For further information contact Gareth Stevens at 1-800-542-2595.

Find us on

PHOTO CREDITS: All images courtesy of Shutterstock. With thanks to Getty Images, Thinkstock Photo and iStockphoto.
Recurring images – Rolau Elena, Chinnisha-Arts, MR. BUDDEE WIANGNGORN, Net Vector, kichikimi, Baskiabat, Perfect_kebab, Receh Lancar Jaya, Mint and Chips. Cover – CRStocker, DedMityay, Elena Istomina, Eric Isselee, Ihor Biliavskyi, MarBom, Tornado_studio. 2–3 – BMJ. 4–5 – F-Focus by Mati Kose, mapman. 6–7 – Arnau Soler, cornfield, avh_vectors, Julian Popov. 8–9 – Eric Carlander, Harry Collins Photography, ianakauri. 10–11 – Archaeopteryx Tours, Ken Donaldson, Vitaly Ilyasov. 12–13 – Maquiladora, Vladimir Kogan Michael, Wang LiQiang. 14–15 – Alfmaler, Attila JANDI, Paul Steven. 16–17 – Barbara Smits, Cristian Puscasu. 18–19 – Colin Edwards Wildside, Giedriius, Tomacco. 20–21 – Andrew Krasovitckii, Astrid Gast, Zacarias da Mata. 22–23 – Adam Hanley, HannaTor.

CONTENTS

Page 4	In the Sky
Page 6	Gulls
Page 8	Sandpipers
Page 10	Oystercatchers
Page 12	Ospreys
Page 14	Puffins
Page 16	Pelicans
Page 18	Sea Eagles
Page 20	Herons
Page 22	Creatures of the Coast
Page 24	Glossary and Index

Words that look like this can be found in the glossary on page 24.

IN THE SKY

The coast is where the land meets the sea.

The coast is home to many interesting and different birds. If you visit the coast, you may see them fishing in the sea, nesting on cliffs, or flying in the sky above the water.

Most coastal birds only live on the coast for part of the year. When the seasons change, they find somewhere else to live. This is called migration.

BARNACLE GEESE MIGRATING

GULLS

LITTLE GULL

HERRING GULL

Gulls are seabirds, often known as seagulls. There are lots of different types of gulls. Some are small, such as the little gull. Others can be large, such as the herring gull.

Most gulls have white, gray, and black feathers. Young gulls often have brown speckled markings. Gulls make their nests on cliffs, sand dunes, and even on the roofs of houses.

KITTIWAKES ARE GULLS THAT NEST ON SEA CLIFFS.

SANDPIPERS

Sandpipers are small to medium-sized birds that live near the shore. They have long beaks that help them find food in the sand. Some sandpipers have long legs, which help them walk along the shore and wade through the water.

Sanderlings looking for food under the sand.

Sandpipers look for food in a few different ways. They will either poke their beaks under wet sand, pick up food from the surface of the sand, or catch insects out of the air.

A sandpiper digging deep into wet sand looking for food.

OYSTERCATCHERS

Oystercatchers are a type of wading bird. Wading birds have long legs. They walk along the sand or in shallow water looking for food. Wading birds, such as oystercatchers, are sometimes known as shorebirds.

Oystercatchers mostly eat shellfish and sometimes worms. Oystercatchers with shorter beaks will hammer their way through shells when eating. Long-beaked oystercatchers will pull the shells open to eat shellfish.

MOST OYSTERCATCHERS DO NOT ACTUALLY EAT OYSTERS VERY OFTEN.

OSPREYS

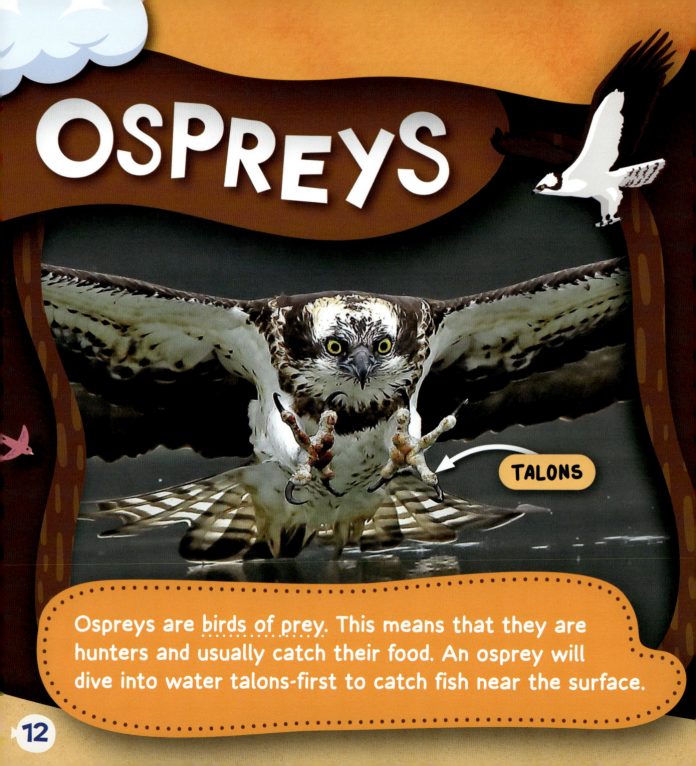

TALONS

Ospreys are birds of prey. This means that they are hunters and usually catch their food. An osprey will dive into water talons-first to catch fish near the surface.

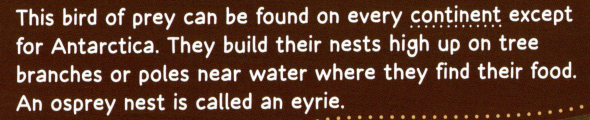

This bird of prey can be found on every continent except for Antarctica. They build their nests high up on tree branches or poles near water where they find their food. An osprey nest is called an eyrie.

OSPREYS GROW TO BE BIGGER THAN GEESE.

PUFFINS

Puffins nest in burrows in the ground.

Puffins are excellent swimmers and spend a lot of time at sea. They are also great at flying. The puffin's strong flying and swimming skills make it an expert at catching fish.

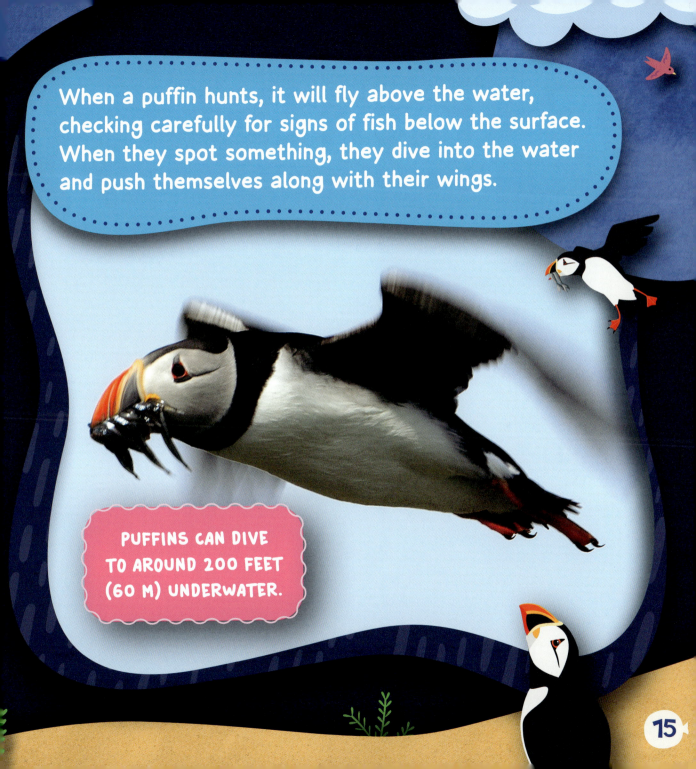

When a puffin hunts, it will fly above the water, checking carefully for signs of fish below the surface. When they spot something, they dive into the water and push themselves along with their wings.

PUFFINS CAN DIVE TO AROUND 200 FEET (60 M) UNDERWATER.

PELICANS

LARGE ELASTIC THROAT POUCH

A PELICAN'S POUCH CAN HOLD ALMOST 4 GALLONS (15 L) OF WATER.

Pelicans are one of the largest birds in the world. Their size is not the only thing that makes them stand out. They have a special elastic throat pouch that they use to catch fish.

Pelicans often work together to hunt for fish. The pelicans will swim around in a circle, forcing the fish together. The pelicans then scoop the fish up with their large beaks.

AMERICAN WHITE PELICANS

SEA EAGLES

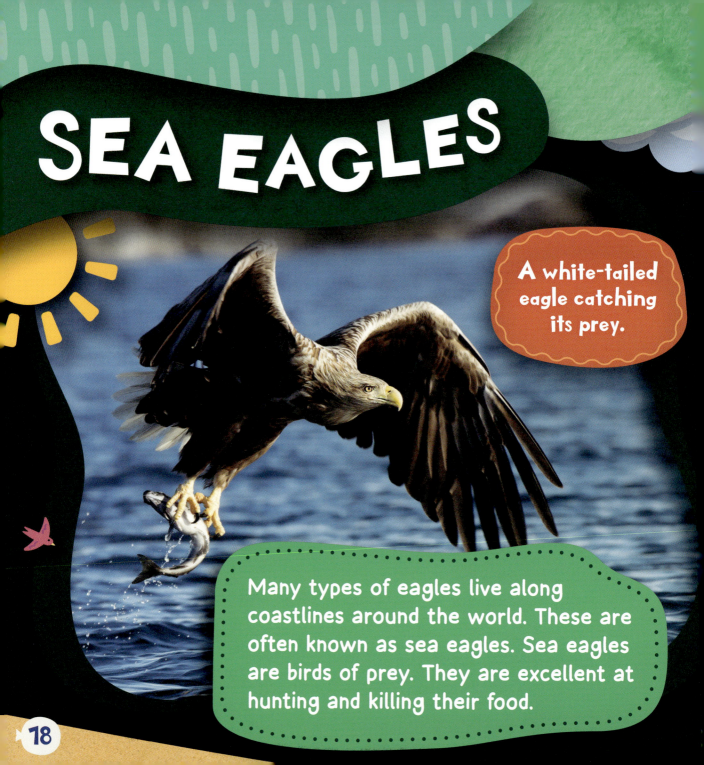

A white-tailed eagle catching its prey.

Many types of eagles live along coastlines around the world. These are often known as sea eagles. Sea eagles are birds of prey. They are excellent at hunting and killing their food.

The bald eagle is a type of sea eagle. Bald eagles mostly eat fish that they catch. However, they will also eat other birds, mammals, and even dead animals that they find.

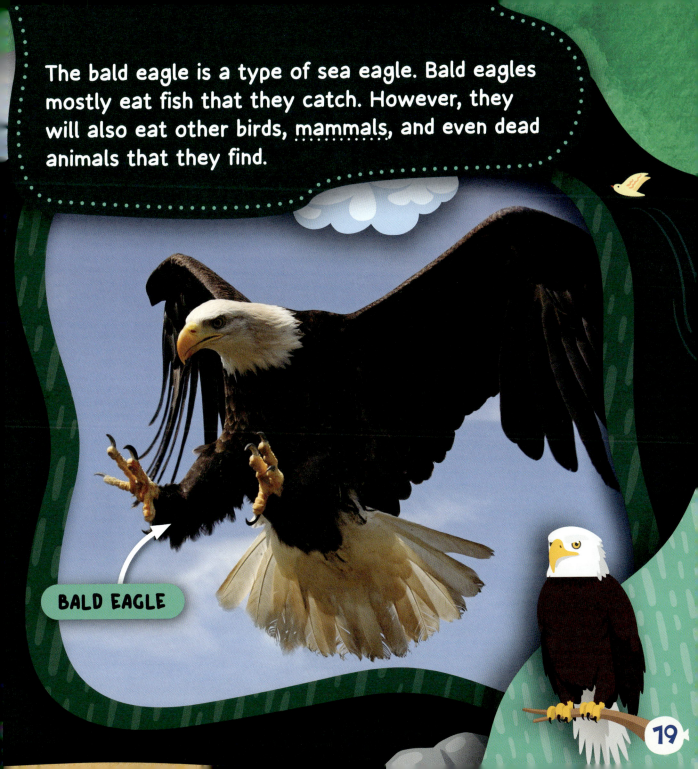

BALD EAGLE

HERONS

HERONS WILL SOMETIMES SPEAR FISH WITH THEIR LONG BEAKS.

Herons are long-legged wading birds. There are many types of herons, but most have long, S-shaped necks and long beaks. Herons hunt by standing very still, waiting for the right moment to strike!

A heron's <u>diet</u> is mostly made up of fish, but they will eat other small animals, such as insects, mice, and frogs. They hunt alone but nest in groups in trees and shrubs.

GREAT GRAY HERON

CREATURES OF THE COAST

The coast is an amazing place to find all sorts of incredible creatures. They are in the sea, the sand, the cliffs, and the skies. The coast gives these animals all the things they need to live.

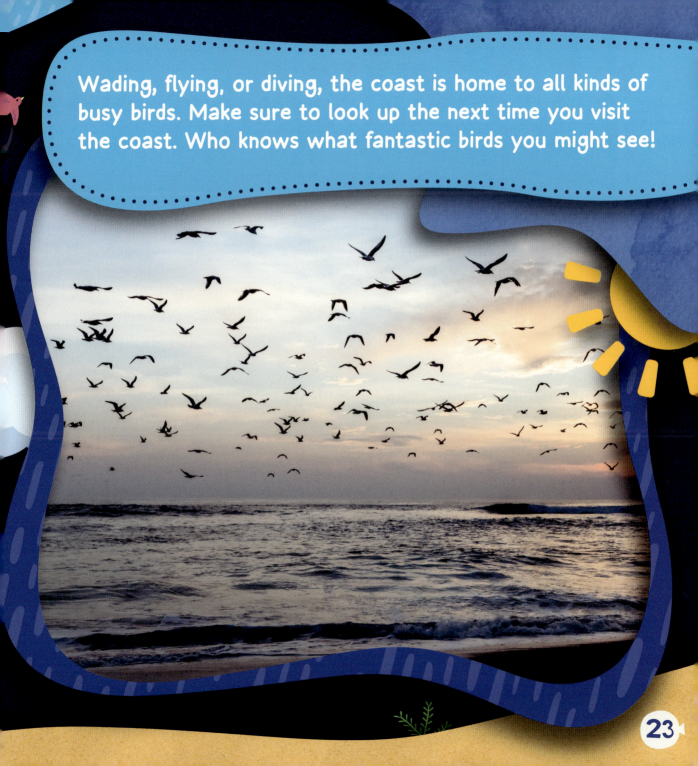

Wading, flying, or diving, the coast is home to all kinds of busy birds. Make sure to look up the next time you visit the coast. Who knows what fantastic birds you might see!

GLOSSARY

birds of prey   birds that hunt and kill their food
burrows   homes made by animals by digging into the ground
continent   a large area of land, such as Africa or Europe, that is usually made up of many countries
diet   the kinds of foods eaten by a person or animal
mammals   animals that are warm-blooded, have a backbone, and produce milk
sand dunes   hills or ridges of sand, formed into a variety of shapes by the wind
shore   the land along the edge of a body of water
shrubs   woody plants that are smaller than trees and usually have many branches coming from near the ground
speckled   markings made up of lots of small spots or patches
strike   to attack quickly

INDEX

beaks 8-9, 11, 17, 20
cliffs 4, 7, 22
feathers 7
fish 12, 14-17, 19-21
food 8-13, 18
nests 4, 7, 13-14, 21
sand 7-10, 22
wading 8, 10, 20, 23